At the Intersection of Existence

At the Intersection of Existence

Davis Stanard

Copyright ©2025 by Davis Stanard

All rights reserved. No part of this publication may be reproduced, distributed, or transmitted in any form or by any means, including photocopying, recording, or other electronic or mechanical methods, without the prior written permission of the author, except in the case of brief quotations embodied in critical articles and reviews.

To M&P, the gift givers;
To C, lover & friend;
To A&F, my joys

Ideas
Truth
God
Purpose
Belief
Life
Death
Immortality
Afterlife
Goodness
Gratitude
Acceptance

Acknowledgments –

Thank you to Camus and Bergman for their insights, and to my wife and brother for their understanding.

Ideas

> "When you go looking for something specific, your chances of finding it are very bad… When you go looking for anything at all, your chances of finding it are very good."

–Bill Pullman, *The Zero Effect*[1]

What is this? The big ideas.
Why write it? To get them out of my head.
Who am I? Nobody.

If you're looking for feel good thoughts, this probably isn't for you. Those offer false comfort. Instead, this is an unflinching look at uncomfortable ideas, absent wishful thinking. Some ideas cast long shadows, which only grow longer the more we ignore them.

I'm no one of note. I have no special expertise or experience, but I've found that often expertise can be a deceit. The topics covered here are both primal and transcendent. The more one studies them, the seemingly less they reveal. Philosophical and theological expertise, intentionally or not, can lead to conceptual rabbit holes, cloaked in fancy words. Trying to understand everything ends up explaining nothing. I'm not going to do that.

My aim is to be as direct and simple as possible, focusing on what can be known. A combination of Occam's Razor[2] – the simplest explanation is usually the right one – and the proverb "If it looks like a duck and quacks like a duck, it's probably a duck." I want this to be like drinking a glass of crystal clear water – absent the flavor of wishful thinking and unclouded by flowery language. And although the following reflects my beliefs, one of those beliefs is that I may be wrong.

Truth

> "It takes two to lie – one to lie and one to listen."

–Homer Simpson, *The Simpsons*[3]

Want the truth?

The drive to learn and understand is a powerful survival tool, allowing us to better manipulate our environment. This drive helps us grow food, build shelter, make weapons, cure illness and so on, allowing us to live longer, compete better, and have more children. So it's only logical that this drive is a product of evolution. Our capacity to observe, deduce, discover and understand is great for figuring out things like how to start a fire – all the way to building elaborate tools to map the vast distances of the universe. Our greatest tool for understanding, the scientific method, is generally based on this framework of observation- and experimentation-based deduction. There's a comforting pragmatism to science that's seductive, leading some to adopt it as their singular belief structure – but it has a blind spot. Some questions it's not designed to answer. Take the question

"Why is there something rather than nothing?" A simple enough question. Science can tell us all kinds of things about *what* things exist, *how* those things are made, and *why* something occurs within a specific context – but on the overarching question of *why* – as in why *anything* exists – it's silent. It's the wrong tool for the question, like tightening a flathead screw with a Phillips screwdriver – you end up going round and round and not getting anywhere. It's incapable of explaining all things. As limited beings, it follows that our tools have limits as well. We are only human, after all.

Our drive to understand is a product of evolution for the purposes of our self-perpetuation. This drive provides tremendous adaptive benefit, however, even after we've managed to feed, clothe, defend and heal ourselves, it runs on. It wants to understand more. It wants to understand *everything* – even when it no longer serves any meaningful purpose. And in this insatiable appetite to understand, some see divine purpose. Why have this unending desire? Well, it must be because there's something out there worth understanding – some greater truth, right? Well, no – not necessarily. We want to know because we have an innate desire to know – but that evolved for survival reasons, not because there's something out there to discover. Maybe there is, and maybe there isn't.

The desire to understand is only satisfied with knowledge – to learn the truth. And to know the truth is to be right. And if you're going to be right, you might as well be certain about it. These are directly connected in a self-reinforcing chain. When an innate desire to understand runs up against questions that can't be easily answered, some search for alternate ways to satisfy this desire. This is when we start to lie to ourselves. We crave knowledge and certainty – even if these "greater truths" don't really impact our lives in any meaningful way. Are we going to eat any better or heal any faster? The crux isn't the questions themselves, but rather why we ask them in the first place. It's an innate desire running past its purpose. When you free yourself from the desire to understand, to know, and to be right, then you free yourself to accept existence as it is.

God

"God is God."

–John Milton, *Paradise Lost*[4]

Are monsters real?

On May 11th, 1996, ValuJet Flight 592 from Miami to Atlanta crashed in a remote area of the Florida Everglades[5]. Imagine you're on that plane. It bursts into flames midair, plummets 7,000 feet and crashes into a swamp. Now let's imagine you miraculously survived that terrifying experience. You're in the middle of nowhere and up to your neck in swamp water, while countless alligators descend upon the crash site, drawn by the terrific commotion. When you're being attacked by a 15 foot aquatic reptile, do you think it really matters what the name we gave it is? And so I ask again – are monsters real?

Words are excellent devices for organization and analysis, but they belong to us, not to the things to which we apply them. Alligator is our label, not the animal's. It doesn't alter the nature of the beast to which it applies. Furthermore, words can obscure the true nature of existence. They're an extension of our desire to understand and know. It isn't a monster – it's just an alligator. It's hard to see past the labels as they so fully define our reality. As useful as they are, they are at the same time masks for reality, obscuring what's right before our eyes.

Words can also create the illusion of division where there is none. Take the case of natural versus artificial – or to frame it slightly differently, nature made versus man-made. Isn't man – humankind – a part of nature? We evolved from animals and are very much a part of this world. Are humans unnatural? Of course not. Some things that appear at first artificial, when viewed from another perspective, reveal themselves otherwise. The built environment may appear unnatural from the human perspective, but zoom out and cities take on an organic shape, like lichen on a rock. The placing of humankind outside the domain of nature is an outgrowth of a religious conceptual framework – an attempt to elevate humankind above the animal kingdom. And it's a self-centered, human way of thinking. Of course there's the understanding of artificial in the sense of synthetic – to replicate something naturally occurring – but again the human element appears to be the distinguishing aspect. We don't consider a mockingbird's calls synthetic or unnatural simply because they replicate other species – why do we consider our replications unnatural? Just because we're human? No, humans – and human behavior and creations – are as natural as anything else. In fact, it's impossible for us to be or do anything unnatural. Natural, unnatural – and for that matter the supernatural (if it indeed exists) – are all a part of the same reality, and therefore are abstract divisions that exist in the mind. Reality itself is not divided – we divide it. In the grand scheme, saccharin is as natural as sugar.

Let's consider the label God. There are many definitions for God, but let's look at the most basic – God, creator of the universe. Compare that to the Big Bang, the event that created the universe. Notice anything? Two labels – similar things. God is a loaded word. Let's set aside our preconceived notions of that word for the moment. When the Bible says "God created man in his own image," *(Holy Bible, Gen. 1.27)* is it possible the reverse is true? That we created God in *our* image – specifically that of a conscious, singular entity? Being human, it's normal we'd project our understanding of being onto God – we project human characteristics onto animate and inanimate things so often we have a word for it – anthropomorphism. But maybe God, if one exists, is nothing like us at all. In the end, there's just one overriding characteristic of an ultimate God – that of creator. And maybe creator and creation, like natural and unnatural, is a division that exists only in our mind.

A scientifically minded person might say that arguing for the existence of God reverses the burden of proof. For example, one might assert that just because there's a lack of evidence of unicorns doesn't mean they don't exist. This places the burden of proof on disproving their existence rather than proving it. Barring any evidence of their existence, the logical conclusion is that unicorns simply don't exist. The difference between belief in unicorns and belief in God is that there's no unexplained evidence of unicorns – there aren't occassional unicorn sightings. But there is unexplained evidence of an all-encompassing creative force – that evidence being the very existence of the universe itself. Even if the universe has always existed, its presence still requires explanation – not of its creation, but of its very being. According to current scientific consensus, the universe is comprised of energy – even matter itself is made of energy[6]. The mere fact that the universe exists, rather than not, is evidence of a massive force – the collective energies of the universe. But if we're following scientific consensus, that also currently points to a creation event.

One moment there was nothing – the next, everything. That requires a staggering creative force. Does it need to grow a white beard and hurl lightening bolts to fit our definition? Maybe it's beyond definition – beyond words. As useful as words are at describing reality, they themselves are not reality. Existence is existence. Or, using John Milton's words, "God is God." We can apply whatever labels we want, but it doesn't change the thing itself.

Purpose

"To be or not to be."

–William Shakespeare, *Hamlet*[7]

What is the primary purpose of a hammer?

I'll give you a hint – it's right in the name. If hammers had emotions, I'm sure they'd feel most fulfilled hammering. What is the primary purpose of life? Again, this shouldn't be hard – it's also right in the name. It's to live. If it does not live, it is not life. Now, *what* a thing's purpose is and *why* its purpose is that – those are two different questions. The hammer was designed by us primarily to hammer things. Its why is clear – *we* are the why. Where does life's why come from? Its why is intrinsic to its very existence. Any life form that does not prioritize self perpetuation and reproduction will cease, and be eliminated from the evolutionary process – a primal law of existence. Our primary purpose is to live and beget life.

If someone does not reproduce, does that mean that they are not fulfilling their purpose? I don't ask this to be cruel, but rather to take an unflinching look at an uncomfortable idea. That said, this is too simplistic. "No man is an island" as John Donne said[8], and to reproduce and perpetuate requires a team approach. Those who do not have children of their own often play important roles in raising others, while medical, educational, charitable, and agricultural undertakings, among others, are important for our continuation. Simply being a productive member of society fulfills needs that allow society at large – and humankind – to prosper and reproduce. Thus, our purpose is fulfilled in a variety of interconnected ways, from direct to more diffuse.

Of course, many people find purpose through artistic, athletic, literary, theatrical, or other undertakings. However, aside from their potential contributions to the perpetuation of our species, they are primarily forms of personal fulfillment rather than a greater, universal purpose.

When some say purpose they mean higher purpose – or meaning. What's the meaning of life? Is there a grander meaning at all? If there is, why isn't it obvious? Let's use Occam's Razor. What's more likely – that someone created all of existence and populated it with living, conscious beings (us), to fulfill some greater purpose – *and then didn't tell us.* Or, there isn't a greater purpose. Draw your own conclusion – unless of course you follow one of the faith traditions, in which case the meaning of life, along with the other 'great questions,' is answered for you.

So, are we nothing more than just a jumble of living cells collected together for adaptive gain, reproducing and spreading wherever we can? Are we nothing beyond the boundaries shaped by evolutionary benefit? Ah, see now we're getting hung up on the *understanding* thing again – our inherent desire to know. Maybe there is more to it, and maybe there isn't, but you don't need to understand your purpose in order to fulfill it. Which is more important? Perhaps fulfilling your purpose is enough.

Belief

> "Faith is believing what you know ain't so."
>
> –Mark Twain, *Notebooks* [9]

What's in the box?

Imagine there's a medium-sized plain cardboard box sitting in front of you. You can't touch it – just look at it. What do you think's inside? It could be anything that might reasonably fit, right? Or it could be nothing. If someone told you the box was filled with money, would you believe them? If you trusted them you might, right? What if that person was a stranger? Either way, the only way to know for certain is to open it and see. Until then, you'll have to take someone else's word for it.

What if someone told you that whatever you believed was in the box was in the box. If you thought it was money, it was money – if you thought it was empty, it was empty. Would you believe them? Of course not. What you believe doesn't change reality – what's inside the box is inside the box, regardless what you believe. What belief does change is *you*. Belief can powerfully affect behavior.

If you believe the box is full of money you'll save it, but if you believe the box is empty you'll end up throwing it away. Same box – but your belief results in opposite actions.

My grandmother raised my father and his three siblings in a small town in rural Illinois. When my father was six, my grandfather left them. Due to the strain, my grandmother had a nervous breakdown. During that time, the Church – she was a devout Catholic – helped look after the family. It was the bedrock upon which she successfully rebuilt her life.

When she was in her mid-70s, a romantic interest from her youth reemerged. Turns out that before she met my grandfather, she had fallen in love with another young man, but her family had opposed the match due to his being Italian Catholic, not Irish Catholic. Now in his elder years, this gentleman had done well for himself. The scent of autumn romance was in the air, and several in the family encouraged her – but to no avail. She steadfastly refused to pursue the relationship on the grounds that she was a married woman. Although she had not seen my grandfather for decades and they were legally divorced (him, long remarried), in the eyes of the Church, she was still married to him.

My grandmother put her faith in the Church, and for very good reason – it was there for her when she needed it most. It gave her a family when her own was falling apart. But later in life, when she had the opportunity for rekindled love, her beliefs became an obstacle.

I'm not questioning the value of any particular set of beliefs but rather focusing on their real impact. Beliefs don't directly change objective reality – they change us. Their value lies in the positive or negative impact they have on us. I'm not suggesting you should believe whatever you want or what you know isn't true, but rather that you *shouldn't* hold beliefs so tightly that they hold you back in life.

Life

"It's a bittersweet symphony, that's life"

−The Verve, "Bitter Sweet Symphony"[10]

How old are you?

The earliest form of life is the single cell organism. These reproduce through single cell division, when one cell splits into two[11]. The original cell doesn't die or disappear – it's the same cell, just two now – twins. Humans reproduce though sexual reproduction involving the combination of an egg with a sperm, and although it's a bit more complicated, the process is still based on cell division[12]. Eggs are formed by splitting – not built from scratch. Everything alive today is connected to those first single cell organisms in an uninterrupted line – alive the whole time. It's like a continuous flame that's been burning – splitting, but not going out – since its inception. The earliest form of single cell organisms appeared on earth four billion years ago. How old are you again?

Maybe you thought you were only several decades old – probably because you were thinking of who you are, versus what you are. What you are is a living thing. Who you are is your conscious self. This second bit is just the latest phase in a very long line – although admittedly a pretty special phase.

Imagine the path life has taken to arrive at you. When a man ejaculates, he releases around 200 million sperm – in one *single* ejaculation[13]. If it wasn't that exact sperm that reached that egg first, you wouldn't exist – a brother or sister would in your place. In just the moment of conception, you were one in 200 million. Now multiply that by the other times your parents tried to conceive – and their parents when they were conceived. And multiply that back for generations since sexual reproduction began two billion years ago. The chance that specifically *you* exist are incomprehensibly unlikely.

Single cell division creates direct, linear blood lines, while sexual reproduction creates a net of interwoven lines – but you're still directly connected to every single one of your ancestors, both animal and human, with an uninterrupted living line. In this sense reincarnation isn't far off the mark. As a living thing you've evolved through countless previous forms – albeit not connected as a consciousness as far as I know.

You might look at this vast net of interconnectedness and see a diminishment of the individual connection, but that is not the case. Imagine incalculable billions of lifelines converging on one spot – that spot is you, at the intersection of existence. If just one of those lines was amiss – poof – you would never have existed. As infinite these lines seem, they are each equally as intimately tethered to your existence.

If you haven't already, I recommend studying your ancestry. It's literally the mapping of this net, bringing this indistinct concept into concrete focus. Your parents, and children if you have them, are your immediate links – singular bonds like no other. Then you have your grandparents, who are a form of parent too – hence the name grand*parents*. All of your ancestors are your grandparents – just a question of how many "greats" to add. With each proceeding generation, the number of grandparents doubles. At 10 generations you have 1,000. At 20 generations, roughly 600 years ago, you have over a million[14].

The Andromeda Galaxy is the farthest object visible to the naked eye[15]. When you look up in the night sky and see its faint glow, you're a being that's been alive for four billion years, transformed from a single cell organism across a spectrum of species into an intelligent life form capable of looking directly at an object that's 15 trillion miles across the universe. As improbable as this sounds, it appears to be the case. Consider yourself lucky.

Death

"I have no secrets."

−Death, *The Seventh Seal* [16]

Have you ever seen someone die?

Let's set aside the question of afterlife for the moment, and take death at face value. By death I mean the common understanding of the term – of the individual, conscious self. Have you ever been with someone when they passed? One moment they're a person, and then they're a thing. It's not really a mystery.

That said, death gets a bad rap. We've turned it into the bogeyman. In reality, death is neutral – the ultimate neutral. If your life is good, then death is a loss, but if your life is suffering, then death is an improvement. It's the zero on the number line – life being comprised of the pluses and minuses. Pain/pleasure, love/hate, yes/no, on/off, hot/cold, yin/yang – these are the ways we experience the world, through myriad shades of positive and negative stimuli and qualities. That includes good and bad – those are qualities one assigns to the lived experience (and to the moment of death, but not death itself). And so, although death itself may not be good, the upside is that it isn't actually bad, either.

You may scoff and say, sure, you say that now but wait until death comes calling – and you're right to. If death is neutral – the ultimate rest – then why are we so afraid of it? We don't fear dreamless sleep, do we? Well, one obvious explanation is that our lives are good and we don't want to give them up. But that doesn't explain our terror of it – what purpose does that serve? Well, actually it serves a very good purpose – survival. How do you motivate something that's alive to keep on living – to spur the hare to outrun the wolf? You make it terrified of dying. Fear is a primal emotion, evolved in us – and animals[17] – to perpetuate life.

Terror of death may lead one to view death as the enemy, but making an enemy of death only ensures one's ultimate defeat. Life and death are not enemies – they're inherently entwined. To die one must first live, and to live is to die eventually. Is a stone dead? No, because it never lived. Life and death spring from the same fountain. They are not separate – they are aspects of the same thing. Life and death form one.

Fear of death has an adaptive benefit – but death is inevitable, so we have a collision of an evolutionary function with an unavoidable reality. There are two things involved here – death, and our fear of it. They are connected, but distinct things. We can't escape death, but we can manage our fear of it. I don't expect to eliminate my fear of death – I still expect to wake in the middle of the night occasionally gripped by it. The shame would be to let that fear significantly negatively impact my life. Don't allow fear of death to define life.

Immortality

"How many vampires do you think have the stamina for immortality?"

–Anne Rice, *Interview with the Vampire* [18]

So you say you want to live forever?

When I was younger, I couldn't understand why you wouldn't want to be a vampire – they're immortal, after all. If one night a vampire came knocking on my window, I'd open it up and stick my neck out. But now I don't think immortality's all it's cracked up to be. The more you think about what true immortality would entail, the less appealing it sounds. What would it feel like to watch all of your loved ones die and the world as you know it be erased by the passage of time? Would you want to stick around for when our sun eventually burns out, throwing our solar system into total darkness? How about when the universe ends – whatever form that takes? When people desire immortality, they're probably thinking it would be one long stretch on the beach – but immortality would be an infinity of agony as well as an infinity of ecstasy. Maybe it's just more life people want. One more year, month, week – just not now, not today. This appears to be driven by fear of dying, rather than desire to live – like a long-distance runner refusing to stop.

Perhaps the goal is to live a long life – but what does that mean? The typical mosquito lives about a week[19]. If it lives a week and a half, it's lived a long time. For humans the average lifespan is about 70 years[20] – if you make it to 100 you're lucky. It used to be 30 – who knows what it will be in the future. Meanwhile, the Methuselah tree in California is 4,853 years old[21] – that's before the Egyptian pyramids were built. Obviously "long" is a relative concept, but whether you live to 70 or 1,000, eventually you're going to die. You can't outrun death – extending your life doesn't change that. Would you rather live a long life or a full one?

Afterlife

> "Let's see what's behind door number two!"
>
> –Monty Hall, *Let's Make a Deal* [22]

Where does the flame go when the candle is blown out?

Afterlife is just a form of immortality. Is there an afterlife? Let's use Occam's Razor again. Which is more likely – when someone dies their soul travels to an invisible world beyond ours from which no one can return and of which we have no evidence? Or when someone dies they're exactly what they look like – dead.

Perhaps it sounds like I'm arguing that there's no afterlife. I am not, because I do not know. The only people who can say for certain are those who have experienced it, and they aren't talking. Whether there's an afterlife or not, what one believes isn't going to change that, so our beliefs have to do with us, not it. If one has an insatiable desire to know, don't worry – that desire will be satisfied. We will in fact discover the answer to this question. So you see, this question takes care of itself, without our help.

When one loses someone close, the thought of being reunited with them one day can be a great comfort, but this doesn't actually require belief in an afterlife. Wherever they have gone, we will follow – whatever form that may take.

Of course there are those who think that what one believes determines what happens – not whether there's an afterlife, but rather if we end up in box or cheap seats. It's hard for me to not see this as a way to convince people to believe in God. Not that I doubt their sincerity, but rather, the temptation to believe in an afterlife can be overwhelming. But God and afterlife, while connected, are distinct beliefs, and should be considered individually. Afterlife requires God, but God does not require afterlife. The temptation of an afterlife clouds vision with self-interest – without it you see clearer.

Regarding what happens when we die, I have my suspicions but not certainty. In the meantime, I'll live as if there is no afterlife and be pleased if I discover otherwise.

Goodness

> "I have always been a man of great principles, but never of great actions."

–Albert Camus, *The Fall* [23]

Are people good?

Depends on your definition of good. If you believe that life is good – specifically human life – then evidence suggests that on balance we are. After all, despite our ups and downs – and we've certainly had our dark chapters – we've managed to increase the quantity of human lives into the billions. In the balance of constructive and destructive tendencies, the scale appears tipped in the favor of the constructive. It takes months of labor and myriad resources to erect a house, but only a can of gas and a few hours to render it to ashes – yet despite this our world is filled with billions of homes. The enormity and complexity of our built environment is a physical manifestation of our on balance goodness by this definition.

But of course that's only good if you're human. What about the greater good, including the collective human, animal and plant kingdoms? In this grander scheme, identifying good is elusive. For the wolf to thrive, the hare must perish. Good and bad becomes a matter of perspective. Does that suggest any behavior can be justified? That is not my intention. I'm merely pointing out that the concept of a universal good founders and crashes against the rocks of reality, whereas human goodness – human truth – is a more productive lens through which to view the issue.

But surely, even in this more limited understanding of 'good,' there are less and more refined forms of it. Is there pure good, true altruism – to do good and sacrifice with no self-interested motivation whatsoever? To which I would ask – why is this important? Where did this measuring stick come from? What does it matter what our motivations are? This is narcissism – it's not the impact that matters, it's what *I think* that's important? This is backwards. Motivations, like beliefs, are for ourselves – actions are for others. Which is better – to do the right thing for the wrong reason, or the wrong thing for the right reason? In short, try to do good, not be good.

Gratitude

> "It's a hell of a thing, killing a man. Takes away all he's got and all he's ever gonna have."

–Clint Eastwood, *Unforgiven*[24]

What did you do to deserve being born?

I don't mean what have you done since you were born – what did you do *before* you were born? Nothing, right? How could you – you didn't exist. So you see, we're born into this life indebted with a gift we didn't earn.

How can we possibly repay such a gift? As Clint Eastwood put it, life is, to paraphrase, "all we've got and all we're ever gonna have." That's not referring to our material possessions so much as all our natural gifts and abilities, joys and sorrows, pleasures and pains – everything that comprises life. Add to this the incredible unlikeliness of being the recipient of such a gift – the chances of our existence being so incalculably improbable as to render the fact that we're one of billions of people statistically insignificant. There are ways to try to repay such a debt – making the most of the our natural talents, living a charitable life, and passing that gift along to the next generation, to name a few. But as wonderful and worthy as these undertakings may be, they cannot fully balance the account.

This is, of course, if one's life is good – we are not all so fortunate. Suffering, grief, and pain are part of life – but for some the physical or mental anguish becomes so great that they decide to return the gift. And for others, the pain is so unbearable that they wish they were never born. For them, what is an incalculably improbable blessing becomes an incalculably improbable curse. But I am not in a position to speak to this, and so can only say that my heart goes out to them.

For those who feel life is a blessing beyond repayment, we are left with accepting the gift with humility and gratitude. It's the gift, quite literally, of everything. Of course if life's a gift it begs the question, who's the giver? But we don't need to know who to thank to be thankful. It's understandable to not want to give up such a gift, but that shouldn't fill us with resentment. Being the recipient of such a gift forever puts us in the positive column in the accounting book of life. Sure, hang onto and care for the gift, but in the end we must return it – it's on loan, not owned.

Acceptance

> "Believe it if you need it,
> Or leave it if you dare"

–The Grateful Dead, "Box of Rain" [25]

Are you at peace?

Perhaps, like myself, you want to know if there's a God, an afterlife, a meaning to life, etcetera, and have spent many hours turning these questions over in your head. Discovering these answers, though, won't change them. Whatever the answers are, they'll remain the same whether we know them or not. The desire to know is about *us*, not them. We may never learn these answers – but we can accept them, whatever they are. We can accept what we do not know.

Or not. We can accept reality as it is – without fully understanding it – or not. But if we do or not is about us. It's my proposition that acceptance may be the most fruitful path to personal peace. If you know a better one, by all means take it.

What about when we lose a loved one? Are we supposed to just accept it? Well, what choice do we have? But don't mistake acceptance for callousness. Acceptance does not prevent grief, despair, or fear – these are unavoidable parts of life if you live long enough. By personal peace, I don't mean the elimination of tragedy or suffering, nor is it my intention to diminish these.

I also don't mean to suggest that accepting reality in this larger sense means we should just accept things as they are in everyday life. We shouldn't stop striving for a better world, an expansion of human knowledge, or a healthier, longer life. If anything, ultimate death – if that in fact is our fate – only makes life all the more precious.

Existence does not need our understanding – we need it. If we let go of this need we free ourselves to accept things as they are – acceptance without total understanding.

Epilogue

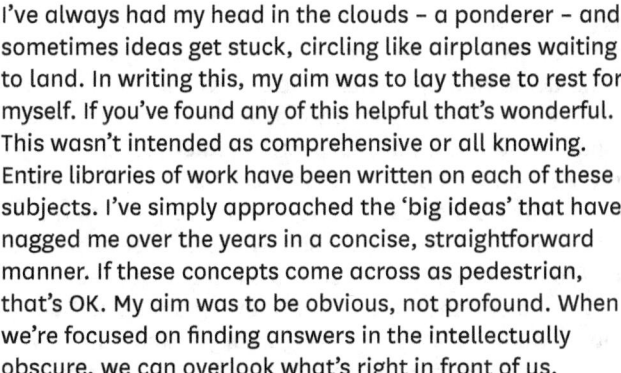

I've always had my head in the clouds – a ponderer – and sometimes ideas get stuck, circling like airplanes waiting to land. In writing this, my aim was to lay these to rest for myself. If you've found any of this helpful that's wonderful. This wasn't intended as comprehensive or all knowing. Entire libraries of work have been written on each of these subjects. I've simply approached the 'big ideas' that have nagged me over the years in a concise, straightforward manner. If these concepts come across as pedestrian, that's OK. My aim was to be obvious, not profound. When we're focused on finding answers in the intellectually obscure, we can overlook what's right in front of us.

I began this book by saying one of my beliefs is that I may be wrong. That's because, despite our certainties, humankind has been proved wrong over and over. We thought the earth was flat, the sun revolved around the earth, we were at the center of the universe, the atom was the smallest particle, time was constant, and so on. Time and again our certainties have fallen – why would the certainties we hold today be an exception? We should continue to strive, learn, and understand – but we should also hold our beliefs with humility, not certainty.

And yet we crave certainty. Uncertainty can be taken as weakness – as though if you aren't certain, you're probably wrong. That and we like to put ideas to bed – especially ones we fear, like death. So we act certain as a defense mechanism. But this kind of certainty is false comfort. Instead of being certain of things we don't know we should accept what we don't know.

I'm an agnostic of sorts and find it amusing the reception this gets from some – almost "pick a side, why don't you." Some view agnosticism as ambivalent – but that is not the case for me. I simply make a distinction between what I know and what I suspect. Whether you think there's a God or not, neither of these beliefs are based on conclusive proof. Religious tradition relies on faith, not evidence, while science simply offers no evidence of God one way or the other. There is a gap between having no evidence of God and knowing there's no God. Mark Twain's "Faith is believing what you know ain't so" may go a bit too far. "Faith is believing what you don't actually know" might be more accurate.

Having faith doesn't mean you're wrong. But more important than being right or wrong is having beliefs that positively impact your life. This is as true for atheists as it is for agnostics and theists. Maybe we'll discover the answer to these questions one day, and maybe we won't. Until then, make the most of life.

References

1. *The Zero Effect.* Directed by Jake Kasdan, performances by Bill Pullman and Ben Stiller, Castle Rock Entertainment, 1998.

2. Ariew, Roger. "Ockham's Razor: A Historical and Philosophical Analysis." *British Journal for the Philosophy of Science*, vol. 47, no. 1, 1996, pp. 117-131, Oxford University Press.

3. "*The Simpsons.*" Created by Matt Groening, performance by Dan Castellaneta, season 2, episode 4, Fox, 1990.

4. Milton, John. *Paradise Lost.* Edited by John Leonard, Penguin Classics, 2003.

5. Dewan, Shaila. "ValuJet Crash: How a Small Airline's Flaws Led to Disaster." *The New York Times*, 12 May 1996, p. A1.

6. Greene, Brian. *The Elegant Universe: Superstrings, Hidden Dimensions, and the Quest for the Ultimate Theory.* W.W. Norton & Company, 1999.

7. Shakespeare, William. *Hamlet.* Edited by David Bevington, Bantam Classic, 1988, Act 3, Scene 1.

8. Donne, John. *Devotions Upon Emergent Occasions*, Meditation 17.

9. Twain, Mark. *Notebooks.* Edited by Fredson Bowers, Volume 2, University of California Press, 1967, p. 345.

10. The Verve. "Bitter Sweet Symphony." *Urban Hymns*, Verve Records, 1997.

11. Campbell, Neil A., et al. *Biology*. 11th ed., Pearson, 2017.

12. Alberts, Bruce, et al. *Molecular Biology of the Cell*. 6th ed., Garland Science, 2014.

13. Williams, Roger, and Richard H. Morrow. *Williams Textbook of Endocrinology*. 14th ed., Elsevier, 2020, pp. 1782-1785.

14. Cavalli-Sforza, Luigi Luca, et al. *The History and Geography of Human Genes*. Princeton University Press, 1994.

15. "Check Out the Hubble Space Telescope's Stunning New View of the Andromeda Galaxy." *Smithsonian Magazine,* 2023, https://www.smithsonianmag.com/smart-news/check-out-the-hubble-space-telescopes-stunning-new-view-of-the-andromeda-galaxy-180985882/.

16. *The Seventh Seal*. Directed by Ingmar Bergman, performances by Bengt Ekerot and Max von Sydow. Svensk Filmindustri, 1957.

17. Panksepp, Jaak. *Affective Neuroscience: The Foundations of Human and Animal Emotions*. Oxford University Press, 1998.

18. Rice, Anne. *Interview with the Vampire.* Ballantine Books, 1976.

19. Service, Michael W. *Medical Entomology for Students.* 4th ed., Cambridge University Press, 2012, pp. 56-58.

20. World Health Organization. *World Health Statistics 2022.* World Health Organization, 2022, pp. 20-22.

21. Fritts, Harold C. *Tree Rings and Climate.* Academic Press, 1976, pp. 112-115.

22. *Let's Make a Deal.* Hosted by Monty Hall, CBS, 22 Dec. 1963.

23. Camus, Albert. *The Fall.* Translated by Justin O'Brien, Alfred A. Knopf, 1957.

24. *Unforgiven.* Directed by Clint Eastwood, performances by Clint Eastwood and Morgan Freeman, Warner Bros., 1992.

25. The Grateful Dead. "Box of Rain." *American Beauty*, Warner Bros. Records, 1970.

www.ingramcontent.com/pod-product-compliance
Lightning Source LLC
Chambersburg PA
CBHW070438010526
44118CB00014B/2096